WHAT WOULD YOUR TEEN LIFE COACH SAY?

A Survival Guide
For Girls Entering High School

Sandra Dupont MA, MS, MFT

WHAT WOULD YOUR TEEN LIFE COACH SAY?
A Survival Guide For Girls Entering High School
© 2010 by Sandra Dupont
All rights reserved

sandra@sandradupontmft.com

Available at www.sandradupontmft.com

The persons, problems and situations presented in this book are fictional. Any resemblance to any actual situation, problem or persons living or dead is coincidental and not intended by the author.

First edition.

This book is dedicated to my nieces
Danielle and Nicole
and to teen girls everywhere.

May you know what it means
to have and be a true friend,
to treat yourself and others with respect
and to live a life of authentic self-expression.

CONTENTS

teendream	ix
Introduction	xi
Puberty – it's freaking me out!	1
Why is my best friend ignoring me?	3
Being popular can be a problem!	5
How do I make friends at my new school?	7
Why are my big sister's friends dissing me?	9
I'm tired of being the younger sister!	11
Why doesn't my mom trust me?	13
How do I deal with summer camp?	15
When will my guy friends grow up?	17
Why am I suddenly nervous around guys?	19
Everyone has a boyfriend except me!	21
Should I tell my boy crush I like him?	23
Why is my boyfriend so possessive?	25
How can I argue effectively with my boyfriend?	27
How can I make my school uniform cuter?	29
How can I act cool when my parents treat me like a baby?	31
What if I don't like my best friend's best friend?	33
Why are other girls jealous of me?	35
Why do people gossip?	37
To be popular, do I have to be mean?	39
But I thought we were friends!	41
Why does my friend say hurtful things to me?	43
How do I stop someone from bullying me?	45

Why don't my parents support my dreams? 47

Why do I feel this need to impress others? 49

Do I have to be perfect to be happy? 51

I'm really struggling with my self-image. 53

Why am I having mood swings? 55

How do I cope with a death in my family? 57

How can I help make this world a better place? 59

Taking your next steps ... 61

teendream
by Maddie Alan Lee

hanging out
that's what we do
pondering glory and greatness,
drinking nostalgia from a plastic cup

that clock ticks,
that song plays,
cross our t's and dot our i's
play fast and loose
eagerly feel up life

say we won't look back,
but do it when we think no one's looking

slip, swallow, sing, startle, emerge
try our very hardest to be unique

and close our eyes so tight
that the blackness deepens around us

make our bodies a smile,
open, and begin again.

Introduction

Around the age of 12, I realized there was a lot about life that I needed to learn: how to handle mean girls, how to talk to my parents, or whether or not to tell a boy I liked him. I was very aware that my life as I knew it was changing, and I wanted to be prepared for the challenges that lie ahead of me. If only there was a way the mature, confident version of myself (that I someday hoped to be) could travel back in time and teach me what I needed to know about overcoming the common pitfalls of being a teenager.

Now, years later, I am a therapist for teenagers. Every day, I listen to the hopes, dreams, fears and concerns of adolescent girls. Drawing from my professional training, as well as my life experience, I coach them on how to deal with the challenges of middle school and high school.

This book is written for girls who want a preview of what to expect and a guide to help them soar through their teen years ...

Sandra Dupont MA, MS, MFT
Teen Therapist/Adolescent Phase of Life Coach

 I'm freaking out! When I look in the mirror, I can practically see my body changing right in front of me. My face is broken out and hair is now growing in places it never did before. I don't think I look as great in my skinny jeans as I used to. I just feel self-conscious, ugly and not myself. I don't know what to do or who to talk to about this. Please help me.

—Poppy, 13

 I can appreciate that you may be feeling scared and overwhelmed by the changes your body is going through. Puberty is definitely a journey into the unknown, and it's filled with new experiences and new feelings.

Childhood was a time of innocence and play. It was also a time of being taken care of by adults. Being a child meant having little to no responsibilities. Becoming an adolescent now requires that you put aside some of your child's play and begin to learn the skills you will need as you get older.

You are not alone. Puberty is a natural part of life that everyone goes through on their way to becoming an adult. During this time, your body is changing in preparation for reproduction and ultimately the creation of a family.

1

I understand the physical changes you are experiencing are causing you stress and concern. It is not uncommon to experience feelings of awkwardness or self-consciousness as you begin looking and feeling differently than you used to. This is where mothers, older siblings and aunts can help. They have already experienced many of the things you are feeling and can step in to guide and support you in the things you need to learn.

Developing a good skin care routine, healthy eating habits, and engaging in moderate daily exercise can help you ease your way through puberty. You might also consider consulting your school nurse to learn more specifically about what you can expect as your body transitions from childhood to adulthood.

 Since my best friend at school has started making friends with some of the popular kids, she's begun ignoring me. When I told her it was bothering me, she said, "That's why I like my popular friends better than you!" And then she ran away, crying. I don't understand. Did I do something wrong?

—Sabrina, 14

 Sometimes our friends make choices that can create distance between them and us. Your friend trying very hard to fit in with popular kids is one example. The problem is that she likes spending time with you, yet dreams of being popular, and this is creating a dilemma for her.

Each of us must ultimately learn whether we prefer having a few close friends or many acquaintances. (Acquaintances are also known as friends of convenience because they're around in the good times, but not necessarily when you need them.) Although you can't make up your friend's mind for her, it sounds like you have a clear idea of the kind of friendship you want with her.

It is understandable that being ignored by your friend is painful. Her reaction to you sharing your feelings indicates that she is struggling with her own feelings. It would be wonderful if the two of you could sit down and talk about what you enjoy about each other. In a perfect world, you would then come to an agreement about how you would like your friendship to be.

It would be ideal if you two could agree that she'll stop ignoring you, and it's okay for her to have new friends. Juggling two sets of friends is possible; however, it will require that both of you act emotionally mature. Unfortunately, not everyone your age is at this level of maturity just yet.

Another option is to spend time with her after school. This will allow you to still be friends while she explores whether the experience of being popular is really what she thinks it is. If this is your choice, you certainly don't want to ruin your time together by complaining.

The last option is to let her move on accepting the fact that sometimes people grow apart. Although you may feel sad, ultimately you need to take care of yourself. If being ignored by her is proving to be too painful, then this could be the best choice.

Being popular has become a problem. At school, only eight people fit at a lunch table. I have more than eight friends so I tend to sit at a different table every day. Some of my friends get upset when I don't sit with them every day or think I'm not sitting with them because I don't like them. I really don't know what to do.

—Yuri, 17

It sounds like you get along with and are well liked by many people, which is a positive thing. It can be challenging, however, when your friends have a different definition of what friendship means than you do.

To some, being a friend means you spend all your time with them. Others may be able to understand that you can have more than one friend or group of friends. It could be helpful to talk to the people who are complaining and find out their definition of friendship.

If your friends are merely feeling a little insecure, re-assuring them that they are important to you may help them let go of their concern that you no longer like them. If they are the possessive type and don't want to share your attention with anyone else, you may need to let them know your definition of friendship is a bit different than theirs.

After talking with them, if there are some who are still being critical of your choices, you'll want to decide if their friendship is worth the price of giving up your other friends to be with them. This is entirely up to you; however, I think it is helpful to hang out with people who are willing to support you and allow you to be yourself.

The bottom line? As much as you might want to, you can't please everyone all the time. You can, however, do your best to be honest and clear about who you are and what you prefer. In this way, the people who are comfortable with your definition of friendship will be happy to spend time with you.

 My life sucks! My father got a new job, and we moved to a different school district. I now live 40 minutes from my old friends, and my parents don't have time to drive me back and forth. I've been keeping in touch with my BFFs by text and Facebook all summer, but they're drifting away.

I started at my new school last week. Nobody seems to want to be my friend. I've tried everything — even giving away my lunch! I act friendly and smile, but people look right through me. When I try to enter into a conversation, I am ignored. I feel invisible. How do I find at least one good friend?

—Poppy, 13

 Getting started at a new school can be difficult. It may seem like everyone already has their friends and aren't open to meeting new people.

You mentioned you would be happy to have at least one good friend. This is a wonderful way to start, and it's definitely an achievable goal.

Start by noticing who looks interesting. Pay attention to what you like about them. Who has friendly eyes? A kind smile? Who is generous to others? Pick at least five people you think might make a good friend. Say hello to them every day for a week and see how they respond. This shows you'd like to get to know them. Their response will tell you who's interested in getting to know you. After you've received a pleasant response from someone, approach him or her to find out more. Introduce yourself, tell them where you moved from, and ask them a question. The question can be about anything, but ideally, find out how they spend their free time.

The secret is to find someone with whom you can have a fun conversation. Lasting friendships are often based on shared interests, meaning that you both like to do similar things. Try asking about their pets, their summer vacation, or their favorite subjects in school. You can also discuss movies you've seen, books you've read, music you like, and even your favorite foods.

Don't settle for someone who isn't that interested in you. Not everyone will be a match. Don't worry about it. Just move on.

Like you said, one good friend is what you would like. And if you find more than one, that's great, too.

 This year I started at the same high school my sister goes to. Her friends are always making fun of me because I'm shy and not outgoing like they are. I don't understand —cuz I've known some of these girls since I was little. When it happens, my sister pretends she doesn't even know me. She used to stick up for me. How can I get her to see how much this hurts?

—Olivia, 15

 I am sorry to hear you are struggling. I imagine your sister loves you as much as she always has, and that she is feeling pressure to fit in with her friends.

Let's think about why people make fun of others. In my experience, people who behave this way are attempting to appear bigger than they are. By picking on someone who is quiet and shy, they believe they can get away with inconsiderate behavior, and they feel more powerful. Their actions speak loudly about their need for approval, which is the opposite of having self-confidence.

Although it would be great if your sister stuck up for you, it's more important that you learn how to handle situations like these. Having a more gentle personality does not mean you're a doormat. When someone says something rude to you, you can respond in a way that you feel good about.

For example, if someone comments on your clothes, you can say something like "Everyone is entitled to their own opinion," or "Thank you for sharing," or "I always wondered what you thought." When you respond in this manner you are not being rude, nor are you showing that their comment hurt you. If you don't give them the reaction they're looking for, picking on you stops being fun.

Instead of complaining to your sister about not sticking up for you, let her know how much you admire and respect her. Ask for her advice on different subjects, and let her take pride in teaching you what she knows. The best way to help your sister overcome her challenge about choosing you or her new friends is to reinforce your relationship with her outside of school.

My sister is three years older than me. My parents let her do anything she wants – going to football games and movies and poetry slams, hanging out with her friends, and staying up late. They never say no to her. It's so unfair!

Why does she get so many special privileges, and I don't get to do anything? I want to do things like that, too. I'm not a baby. Why do they treat me like one? I'm so angry I could scream!

—Poppy, 13

 The first thing you need to understand is that your sister is not to blame for the privileges she gets for being older. It's a big job for parents to decide when their child is ready for certain activities or responsibilities. This has nothing to do with their love for either of you and has everything to do with making wise decisions about their children's safety. Getting angry with your sister won't help. Because she is older, she can teach you a lot of things that will make your life easier. At the very least, you can learn by watching her. Ideally, she will be a friend for the rest of your life.

Try one of these stress reducers when you're feeling upset:

- Politely ask your parents when they think you

might be able to participate in the activity you are feeling jealous about.

- Start a gratitude journal. Before going to sleep, write down at least five wonderful things that happened that day. (Share this with your parents if you want.)
- Take a deep breath. Remind yourself that your family loves you very much, and that when your sister was your age, she had the same limitations that you do now.
- Avoid comparing yourself to anyone else. Instead, live every moment enjoying what you have and what you do.

Remember, younger sisters get cool perks that older sisters don't get anymore! Maybe your mom does your laundry, but your older sister has to do her own. Soon you'll be old enough to get the privileges your sister gets – something you can look forward to.

 My mom is driving me crazy. She's always in my face, asking me who I'm talking with on the phone and what I'm doing on the computer. She literally hovers over me. I'm older now, and I want my privacy. What's her deal? Why doesn't she trust me?

—Megan, 15

 Parents often struggle to balance giving their children the freedom to make choices (and experience the natural consequences of their behavior) with the responsibility of teaching their children about life, all the while keeping them safe.

It sounds like you feel hurt that your mom checks up on you. Her questioning your integrity may conflict with your self-image and the way you would like to be perceived.

Raising a child today isn't easy. The Internet allows kids to connect with people they might not otherwise meet. Having a cell phone allows kids to talk 24/7 without parental supervision. This is terrifying for parents, who want to protect their children.

Trust is something that is earned. When you answer your mother's questions, you help her to recognize you are making mature and responsible choices. Try talking with her about her fears and your desire to earn her trust. Ask what she needs you to do to in order for you to gain more freedom.

If you show her you have nothing to hide, in time she may relax. If, however, you are doing things you shouldn't be doing, as frustrating as it may be, your mom is really doing you a huge favor. Adolescence is a time of exploration, and unfortunately, it's not uncommon for teens to make unsafe choices.

If, however, you are doing everything she is asking you to do, but it still feels like she's micromanaging your life, you may be dealing with a particular parenting style. Some parents are just anxious. Unfortunately, like a personality style, it won't change easily. In this situation, the best advice I can give you is to be patient with her and try not to take her questions personally.

 My parents are sending me to a sleepover camp in the mountains this summer. I'm excited. I know it's going to be super fun, but now that I'm actually going, I'm feeling anxious and nervous. I won't know anybody. I'll be there for a whole month — I've never been away from home or my best friends. I'm really worried I'll be homesick. Help!

—Poppy, 13

 Traveling alone for the first time and leaving behind everything that is familiar can be scary. You don't know what to expect and aren't sure how people are going to respond to you. It can also be exciting and rewarding. Adventure and the possibility of new friendships await you!

Summer camp is an opportunity to practice your social skills and experience new things. By stepping out of your normal routine, you have the opportunity to grow as a person. When you return to school in the fall, you'll be richer for all the things you've learned.

One way to deal with being homesick is to bring something with you that feels comforting. How about a pillowcase with a photo of your family on it or some pre-addressed note cards so you can send letters filled with stories of your adventures to your family and friends? At the very least, a couple of photos of your family, friends and pets can be looked at whenever you want and shared with people you meet.

The first day of camp is often like the first day back at school after summer vacation. People who know each other will gather together and visit. See what group looks interesting and go introduce yourself. There will also be other new people like yourself who could be open to getting to know you.

Participate in all the activities. Avoid making snap judgments about people. Give yourself permission to enjoy yourself and take it all in. It's okay to be silly. It's okay to have fun. Spend time with people who make you laugh. Summer camp is meant to be a break from school, so don't worry about doing everything perfectly.

A big key is your attitude. Kindness and a sense of humor can go a long way toward making new friends.

 My guy friends at school treat me like one of the boys. We used to have fun doing stuff together, but now they're always teasing me and playing practical jokes. Sometimes if I wear a headband, they'll take it from me and take turns wearing it and acting like me. If I ask them to stop, they just do it more. It used to be funny, but now it's embarrassing. I feel like they don't respect my feelings at all. What's their problem? Why don't they grow up?

—Poppy, 13

 It can be aggravating when guy friends tease you, but did you know that teasing is a common form of play among guys? If you observe groups of guys who are friends, whether they're young or old, you'll often hear them teasing each other. If your guy friends are teasing you, it means they like you.

At a certain age, being treated with respect becomes very important to girls. Adolescence is a time when girls and guys start practicing more grown up behavior. During this time, however, girls tend to mature faster than their male friends. Thus, your guy friends might still treat you like one of the boys instead of the way you would prefer to be treated.

17

If the teasing is getting to be too much for you, consider setting boundaries. This means politely excusing yourself from situations in which you feel uncomfortable. Essentially, you are giving them a clear message that their behavior is not okay with you.

Only you can decide what behavior you are willing to tolerate. The good news is that as your male friends get older, they will put more effort into trying to please you. The key is to communicate your feelings politely and openly.

Girls and guys often see the world differently. It is important to remember that during adolescence, you are learning about each other through your interactions. Patience, kindness and forgiveness go a long way toward having positive experiences with boys. At the same time, you have the right to decide how you want to be treated. It's up to you to choose your friends wisely.

 I've always had guy friends, but recently every time I see one of the boys I've known since kindergarten, I get butterflies in my stomach. When he talks to me, I either say stupid random stuff or I get all tongue-tied and can't talk at all. Sometimes I sound like I'm speaking a different language. Something is seriously wrong with me. What is going on?

—Sophia, 14

 There isn't anything wrong with you. You're in a new phase of life, and your relationships with guys are changing.

If you get those butterflies in your stomach every time you're around a certain guy, it's a sign you're attracted to him — you just don't recognize what that feels like yet. What you are feeling is not at all unusual. As your hormone levels change, you can become biologically interested in those who could be potential life partners, which may leave you feeling self-conscious around those who, up to now, were simply your friends.

As you grow up, you won't necessarily continue talking about the things you used to talk about when you were a child. As a result, you will also find yourself struggling to interact with old friends in new ways. These situations can leave you feeling awkward as you ramble on, or embarrassed when your mind suddenly goes blank in the middle of a sentence.

Lastly, boys and girls who played together as children can start developing new areas of interest as they prepare for their roles as young men and women. Our society tends to define people in terms of male and female roles with different sets of expectations for each. This can be confusing, as those roles are not so obvious when we are children. People we thought we knew well can suddenly feel like strangers as their interests move in new directions.

Your responsibility during this time is to discover who you are and who you like spending time with. Start by choosing companions with whom you feel you can completely be yourself.

 Suddenly it seems like everyone except me has a boyfriend. Even my little sister has a guy calling her! My friends are all changing — all they want to do now is hang out with their boyfriends or talk about how great their boyfriends are. I feel sad and very alone. Yet, I don't feel ready to start dating. What should I do?

—Sabrina, 14

 Change is not easy for anyone. Watching your female friends start putting their energy and attention into guys can definitely leave you feeling left out, especially when you do not feel ready to join them. You can be one age physically, but feel emotionally younger.

As your relationships with your friends change, the closeness you once felt is not there in the same way anymore. You are basically experiencing the loss of something you value. Understandably, this can be a sad time. But this does not mean that your friends no longer care about you.

Growing up is often filled with change: new schools, body changes, meeting new people, saying goodbye to people you liked, and starting to date. Change often means the loss of familiar things; however, change, although challenging, can also bring exciting new beginnings.

The time when girls and guys begin dating does not happen the same way for everyone. Some girls jump right in, while others prefer to take things slower. There is nothing wrong with waiting until you feel ready. In fact, it is wise to listen to your inner wisdom about what is right for you. Eventually, most everyone begins to explore this new phase of life.

Something that can help you during this transition is to become a good listener to your friends. They will want to share their adventures in dating, and you can definitely learn from their experiences. Listening is also a good way to stay connected and show you care.

Friendships, like any relationship, evolve over time. The key to keeping a relationship alive and healthy is to give each other space to grow and change. So, remember to spend time participating in activities you enjoy, while you give your friends space and time to find their way.

 I have a crush on the guy who sits behind me in Spanish class. He doesn't know. (At least I don't think he does!) Should I say something or just keep hoping he'll notice me? What if he never does? Or what if I tell him I like him, and he doesn't like me back?

—Sophia, 14

 Boys usually start getting interested in girls around middle school. If a guy likes you, he is probably going to show it. Look for signs like whether he teases you (kindly) or pays attention to you. Since girls act more mature than guys at this age, don't be surprised if he gets uncomfortable when he finds out you like him. He's probably worried about what his buddies will think of him.

A lot of kids prefer to hang out in groups. This allows you to be around people you like without feeling pressured or awkward. High school is a great time to become friends with guys and learn who you feel comfortable around. Do you like being around funny and playful guys, or do you prefer someone who is extremely smart? Does it matter if he is drop dead gorgeous if he isn't kind-hearted?

Don't be in a rush to find someone to be with just because your friends have boyfriends. If the guy you like does not show interest in you, move on. Not everyone is going to appreciate your charm and beauty.

If you like someone, just act normal. Smile and say hi when you see him. If he asks you a question, be friendly and create a conversation. Find out about his hobbies or what he likes to do with his weekends. Get to know him better.

What you really want to know is if you enjoy each other's company and if he treats you with respect. Remember to always take good care of your feelings by choosing to be with guys who you consider to be true friends.

 My new boyfriend wants to be with me all the time. When I hang out with my friends, he calls or texts me to ask what I'm doing and who I'm with. Once I even caught him spying on me when I was at the mall with my BFF! At first it made me feel special, but it's starting to bug me. I like him, and I like spending time with him, but I don't want to be with him every second of the day. Plus, my friendships are important to me. What can I do to get him to stop acting so possessive?

—Yuri, 17

 It sounds like it's time to have a talk with your boyfriend about your relationship. When you come together as unique individuals, you bring hopes and expectations of what you want from your partner with you. Not everyone has the same definition of what being a couple means.

It's not uncommon for young people to want their partner's undivided attention. Having a girlfriend like you could be a real boost to your boyfriend's self esteem. This could lead to him feeling protective of his relationship, and possessive of you; however, when his wants conflict with your needs, it is not a healthy situation.

Early in a relationship is a good time for

couples to think about and agree upon guidelines for their relationship. Do you want to spend 24/7 together? Or would you prefer to hang out in groups or on the weekends?

Each person has their own idea of what they want the relationship to look like. For example, you might want to hang out with your boyfriend on the weekends, but focus on your studies and be with your girlfriends during the week. He, on the other hand, might not have as many activities and could feel jealous of the time you spend with others. It is important to re-assure him that even though you want to spend time with your friends, you still care about him.

No one owns another human being. Essentially you need to be with someone who is willing to give you space to be yourself and feel comfortable within the relationship. I suggest talking to him about finding a middle ground between your differing wants and needs.

 When my boyfriend and I argue, which is not that often, he interrupts me and tries to change my mind. It makes me frustrated. He never stays on topic and is always talking in generalizations. I feel like he is more concerned about winning the argument than actually listening to me. What can I do to get my point across?

—Chloe, 17

 It can feel frustrating when you don't feel heard. People often get passionate when expressing their opinion, and even people who get along well most of the time can have disagreements; however, it is possible for each of you to express your feelings without alienating the other person. Here's how:

First and foremost, it is essential to really listen when he is speaking instead of preparing your response in your head. Stick to the topic you are discussing; don't jump all over the place or bring up past hurts or misunderstandings. Try to see his point of view. Be willing to admit when he is making a good point and be open to finding a compromise. Sincerely apologize when you realize you are wrong.

Arguing respectfully means not raising your voice, swearing, calling each other names, or wagging your finger in the other person's face. Threats and taunting will only escalate the tension between you. Healthy relationships are based on honesty and trust, so don't ever lie or exaggerate to make your point.

You should not put yourself in a position where you fear the argument could get physical. Laying a hand on a partner in anger is never okay. Therefore, decide upon a safety phrase or gesture that indicates you need a "time out" if an argument gets too heated. You can always resume the discussion at a different time when you both are calmer.

These suggestions work best when both partners agree to use them. It's easier to be heard when expressing your opinion thoughtfully and respectfully. Mutual respect is at the heart of any good relationship. And remember, another option is simply to agree to disagree.

My school has a dress code and my school uniform is ugly. I'd really like to wear cute outfits like the popular girls but still follow the dress code. I don't want to look like everyone else. I want to express myself. I just don't know how to do it. Could you give me some suggestions?

—Olivia, 15

 School uniforms are basically designed to make everyone look similar. The fact that you want to follow the dress code shows respect for your school. Your parents and teachers will appreciate that, and in return, they'll treat you with respect.

The nice thing about wearing a school uniform is that you don't have to stress out about what you are going to wear every day. It also takes the pressure off of having to own all the latest fashions and allows girls with more limited budgets to feel comfortable. The hope is that students will focus more on school than on what they are wearing.

That being said, you don't have to look like everyone else. It is important to find a creative expression that feels right for you. Clothing is one of the many ways you can use to express your unique personality.

Since adolescence is a time when boys and

girls start checking each other out, girls may attempt to stand out in different ways. Some girls do this by wearing clothes that attract attention. What kind of attention do you imagine the outfits worn by the popular girls attract? Is that the kind of attention you want, or are you looking for something else?

As for looking cute, there are many creative ways to approach that goal. It could be fun to start a new trend by wearing something that nobody else is wearing. There may be options for self-expression in the way you wear your hair (adding headbands, bows or other ornaments) as well as accessorizing with bracelets, necklaces, leggings, tights and shoes.

It is important to find a style that feels right for you. You don't necessarily have to look like everyone else; however, clothing is just one of the ways that you can express the unique person that you are. A wise person once told me, "One of the best thing to wear to school and really stand out is a smile."

My parents make me go to bed early, while my friends get to stay up late and watch all the cool shows. Then the next day at school, when they're all talking about them and what's going to happen the following week, I have no idea what's going on! I'm embarrassed that I have to go to bed so early. I'd just die if anyone found out. Should I just keep playing it cool and pretend to know what they're talking about?

—Sophia, 14

 Your question is about more than television shows. Let me share a simple truth: your friends are also trying to look cool while dealing with the limits their parents set.

Adolescence is a time for discovering who you are and how you want to be perceived in the world. One of the challenges every teen faces during this time is dealing with their family's unique rules. The key is to respond with respect and creativity. Politely explain the situation to your parents, and ask how you can earn the privilege of staying up a little later.

Some shows that are on late at night have adult language and situations that some parents do not want their children exposed to. It could be helpful to hear your parents' opinions about the shows

31

you'd like to watch. If they're open to you watching these shows, but are concerned about you getting enough sleep on a school night, perhaps they'll consider recording them for viewing the following day or on the weekend.

It's likely that there will be times you will not be allowed to do things your friends are doing. As long as you live in your parents' house, they will be setting the rules. The better relationship you have with your parents, the better your chance of negotiating for the things you want. And when you don't get your way, try to remember you are not the only one whose parents set limits.

As for the conversations with your friends, you don't have to pretend you know what they're talking about. Neither do you have to reveal your bedtime. Don't feel like you have to participate in every conversation. Sometimes it's enough to just sit back, listen carefully and enjoy the moment.

 I'm confused. I like my best friend, Anna, a lot. But Hannah, who is Anna's best friend, is someone I don't trust — she has lied to me in the past, and sometimes she just ignores me. I'm beginning to want to avoid Anna because of the way Hannah acts, but I don't want to hurt Anna. What should I do?

—Sabrina, 14

 You mentioned that you and Hannah are best friends with Anna. Sometimes when a person has more than one best friend, her friends may compete for her attention.

It sounds like you don't enjoy your time with Anna as much when Hannah is around. Given the fact that she has ignored you and has even lied to you, I can appreciate why you feel you can't trust her.

Let's consider some options. You could, as you suggested, stop being Anna's best friend. But as you said, you don't want to hurt Anna, and she isn't the one you're having problems with.

Sometimes, it can be helpful to add more people to the equation. When there are only three of you, if Hannah is talking to Anna, you have no one to talk to. But with even one additional person present, the situation becomes more balanced.

Another option is to invite Anna to spend time alone with you. At school this may not be easy to do, but after school and on weekends, she may be willing to set aside time to be with you.

And although perhaps not your first choice, a third option is to find a way to get closer to Hannah. If you have both been competing for Anna's attention, it's possible your friendship has never had a chance to grow. If you can figure out how to make Hannah a good friend, this could entirely solve your problem.

In life, we will not necessarily like everyone we meet, nor will everyone like us. People may change over time, as may friendships. If you currently enjoy Anna's company and are not ready to give up your friendship, it's up to you to find a creative way to deal with her having other friends. Perhaps you might want to add a new friend or two to your life.

 I'm a cheerleader. Some of my friends act totally jealous because I can do flips and stuff that they can't. It's not my fault that I'm good at it — I used to take gymnastics. They think I'm showing off, but I'm not like that. When I tell them I'm just practicing, they just roll their eyes. Why are they behaving that way?

—Yuri, 17

 What you are describing is called envy. Sometimes, when you have something someone else wants, they attempt to take it away from you by putting it (or you) down. This is one reason that gossip magazines and entertainment shows are so popular. Everyone seems to want to hear the dirt on people who appear to live a perfect life.

You have choices here:

- You can keep doing what you are doing with the understanding that other girls may act envious.
- You can stop doing your cool tricks and anything else that makes you stand out.
- You can share what you have by helping those who are interested learn how to do gymnastic tricks of their own.

It's not uncommon for teenage girls to pick on

others who stand out from the crowd. Adolescence is a time of competition. As girls compare themselves with others, someone who may be taking attention away from them can be perceived as a threat.

I recommend sharing as a way to build a bridge between you and those who wish they had what you have. Of course, there may still be some who won't accept your gift, but there will be those who will realize what a sincere and nice person you are. In time, ideally, these girls will come to realize you each have your own unique place in this world, and one person's success does not necessarily mean another's loss.

To have good friends you first need to be a good friend. Good friends share what they have. Good friends stick up for each other. Good friends are kind to each other. Good friends encourage each other to be the best they can be. Lead by example, and be the kind of friend you would like to have.

 My best friend does a lot of gossiping and trash talking about others. It makes me wonder if she's discussing me when I'm not around. I don't know if she likes the drama or what, but I'm about ready to just walk away — I'm getting tired of her mean and critical comments.

—Tiffany, 16

 It's always fun to get together with friends and chat about things, even other people, but crossing the line to gossiping can be problematic. It can ruin reputations, not only for the person being talked about, but also the person who is spreading the rumors. It is helpful to try to understand why people gossip.

- Your friend could be feeling envious or jealous of the person she is gossiping about and is saying negative things about that person to feel better about herself.
- She may be trying to become more popular by using gossip as a way to gather people around her.
- She may be angry with someone, but instead of handling her hurt feelings directly with that person, she is venting her feelings publicly.

- She may not approve of the person's behavior and is trying to influence that person to change by alerting everyone to what he or she has done.

Since she is your best friend, your opinion is probably important to her. Have you considered sharing your feelings and concerns about gossiping? This could create an opportunity for a discussion. If she seems open to discussing the subject, you could even express your fear that she is talking about you to others. You can then invite her to tell you directly about anything she thinks is getting in the way of your friendship and promise to do the same for her.

She is doing what she is doing for a reason; however, she may not understand why she is doing it. Your conversation could be a safe place for her to explore her feelings. Together, you might discover better ways than gossiping to handle the situation.

 Many of the popular girls at my school are also known as mean girls. I don't get it. Is that some kind of requirement for being popular? I'd like to be popular, but I'm wondering, is it possible to be popular without being mean?

—Yuri, 17

 First, let's look at your definition of popular. Does it mean a lot of people know who you are and are constantly competing for your attention and approval? Or does it mean that you are trustworthy and fair, a person others look up to for your wisdom, support and great sense of humor?

I imagine you have an idea of how your life would be different, and somehow better, if you became more popular. It might be helpful to write down the things you think you would gain by becoming popular as well as a list of things you might also need to give up in order to achieve that status.

Does being popular mean you will always have to be concerned with how you look or what other people are saying about you? Would you need to engage in gossiping or being cruel to others? Would you be constantly obsessing over whether someone else is more popular than you? How would you know who your true friends really are?

Second, when someone is consistently acting mean to others it is often an indication that they are not happy inside. People who choose to be hurtful and rejecting of others are probably struggling with some insecurity they try to hide by appearing tough or overly confident.

Not everyone handles popularity the same. Being popular can actually be an opportunity to make a positive difference in your world. Like celebrities who use their influence to help those in need or draw attention to important causes, you too could be a positive role model, someone your classmates turn to and aspire to be. And if you choose to pursue popularity, please don't forget the people who already love you for who you are.

 I feel so hurt. Today at school I over-heard some friends talking about how much fun they'd had at the birthday party of my closest friend. I can't believe it — not only did she not invite me to her party, she didn't even tell me she was having one! I don't know what to do. I thought we were good friends. Is she trying to tell me that she doesn't want to be my friend any more?

—Sophia, 14

 I understand that you must be feeling sad about being excluded from your friend's birthday celebration. There could be a number of possible reasons why she didn't invite you. A few that come to mind are:

- Her parents told her she could only invite a certain number of guests and she picked a group she thought would get along well to-gether.
- She may not feel as close to you as you feel to her.
- She may be angry over something that hap-pened between the two of you that you didn't realize upset her.
- She may have decided to move on to a new group of friends.

Middle school can be a time when people change friends frequently as they attempt to figure out who they are and with whom they want to spend time. Some people call everyone they know a "friend," when they actually just happen to be in the same grade or class together.

There is a significant difference between acquaintances and true friends. A true friend is someone who repeatedly shows you, over time, that they want to be with you. My questions to you are: How long have you known her? And do you feel comfortable enough asking her why she didn't invite you to her party?

A true friend is also someone with whom you can talk to about these types of situations and work things out. Her answer to your question will tell you whether or not she is indeed a true friend.

If, in fact, you learn she doesn't really want to be your friend, it's time to move on and find someone who does. You deserve to be with people who enjoy your company and will stand by you.

 I joined a basketball league this year. Last week my BFF and I were at her house shooting hoops and she declared she was a better player than me. Maybe that's true, but did she have to come right out and say it? Now I feel uncomfortable around her. She really hurt my feelings.

—Olivia, 15

 I can appreciate that what your friend said about being better than you, at a sport you now compete in, did not feel good. Since you are BFFs, let her know how you feel.

The problem isn't that she thinks she is a better player; it's more that she didn't understand how her words affected you.

What did her words mean to you? Did they mean she doesn't care about you the way you thought she did? That you are not her equal? To be able to communicate what you feel, it is important for you to first understand what you are feeling.

During adolescence teens are trying to figure out who they are. By comparing yourself to others, you can find out what you are good at and where you have to work harder. Your friend may have simply been trying to feel good about herself.

Adolescence is also a time of feeling vulnerable and insecure, which is why teens can be very sensitive to things their friends say. This may be why it feels awkward to be with her right now.

Something else to consider is that there are often unconscious expectations that go together with being best friends. One example is that a best friend cheers you on and believes in you. It can be shocking and disappointing when a friend is less than positive or encouraging.

By kindly and respectfully communicating your feelings, you can help repair this situation. Your friend may not have meant any harm. She may even believe that you are better than her in other areas. Use this as an opportunity to strengthen your friendship by discussing what it actually means to be best friends.

I'm being bullied at my school but am too afraid to tell a teacher or friend for fear it might make it worse. I am not being physically hurt, but their insults are really mean. I've become scared to go to school and I don't know what to do. They say horrible things to me and then make me promise not to tell anyone. What can I do to make them stop?

—Sabrina, 14

 There is a very old saying that goes "Sticks and stones may break my bones, but words can never hurt me." Of course words can hurt your feelings! But what this means is you have a choice over whether the words said about you, hurt you. Did you know that your thoughts about the words are what give the words the power to hurt? Therefore, words can only hurt if you let them.

The purpose of someone saying mean things to you is to upset you. My question to you is do you think what they are saying about you is true? If not, then try pretending you didn't hear it and just walk away. If the insult is about something true, try finding humor in it. Nobody is perfect, and we all have our little imperfections and faults. One way to get around the challenge of mean words is to not take them seriously.

Unfortunately, name-calling is a very normal childhood experience, which can continue into adulthood. Freedom of speech is one of the rights we have in our country. Therefore, it is extremely helpful to develop a good sense of humor and be able to joke about yourself.

By using an adult to stop a bully from saying hurtful things to you, the bully may get angry and try to retaliate by taunting you even more. The way to make a bully stop teasing you is to not give them the satisfaction of seeing that their words upset you. This takes away their sense of power over you.

Just know that the teasing may get worse before it gets better, because the bullies will test you to see if they can make you react. The key to your success is to be totally consistent in how you respond.

 My parents NEVER support me except in schoolwork and things THEY are interested in. I want to be an actress and singer, but my mom won't sign me up for lessons or let me audition for a play. Why won't they support me in what I want? Can't they see I have my own dreams?

—Megan, 15

 In an attempt to protect their children from disappointment, parents often try steering them toward careers with which they themselves are more familiar and comfortable. The entertainment industry is highly competitive. The hours required to be successful in that profession can take away time from school, friendships and other social activities.

It sounds like your parents have strong ideas about what it means to be an actor or singer. They may be concerned that if all your energy is focused on being in the entertainment industry, you will miss out on other experiences. It might be helpful to sit down with them and discuss their concerns.

If you are respectful when listening to them, you may find that they may be more open to hearing your request for acting lessons. Expressing your interests in a mature manner will get you much closer toward your goal than sulking or storming around the house. See if your parents are willing to meet you half way. For example, perhaps they would be open to you taking an acting class provided that you maintain a certain GPA, and/or participate in another activity of their choosing.

Joining school singing and theatre groups is a good way to gain experience and prove that your passion for the performing arts is serious. As time passes, your parents may discover that you have the talent and commitment to go the distance as a singer or actress. In the meantime, there is value in participating in a variety of experiences and meeting different types of people, as the information could come in handy in a future acting role that you might someday be asked to play.

When I was younger, I had my own style and I didn't care what other people thought. Lately I find myself dressing and doing things to try to get people to like me or pay attention to me, but then end up not feeling good about myself. Why do I do this?

—Tiffany, 16

If you dress to impress, say things that don't represent your true feelings or pretend to be someone you're not, let me share a story with you.

Once there was a lion cub that got separated from his family. He was adopted by a flock of sheep and lived with them comfortably for many years. They ate grass, slept and avoided predators together.

The cub grew into an adolescent. One day while he was exploring a pond, a mature lion walked up and asked him what he was doing by himself. The cub shook, looked for an escape, and replied, "Bah. Bah."

The mature lion then invited the young lion to look in the pond at the image of them side by side.

When he did, the adolescent realized he was not a sheep at all, and with a little encouragement from the elder, he threw back his head and roared.

This is a story about finding your authentic expression. We come into this world with unique gifts and talents, each with our own physical expression, personality and style. Add to that our life experiences and interests, and we are like no other.

Adolescence is a time of self-exploration. By trying on various types of behavior, you can explore your authentic expression. Are you an athlete? A scholar? A clown? A peacemaker? These are questions only you can answer.

Think about how you would like your future life to be. For some, this might mean raising children in a love-filled home. For others, it could mean becoming educators and contributing to changing the world. Anything is possible. First, you must get to know yourself, and then develop the confidence to be yourself in all your magnificence.

I encourage you to discover your authentic expression so that you too may throw back your head and roar.

Why is life so hard? I spend too much time trying to make other people happy — my parents, my friends, my boyfriend. I feel pressure to live up to other people's expectations, and I'm always apologizing when I fail to do so. Sometimes I don't seem to know who I am or what I want. Why is it such a struggle to just be myself?

—Chloe, 17

 Your question addresses many reoccurring adolescent themes: the struggle for perfection; wanting to please everyone and losing yourself in the process; feeling angry, but not having the skills to express yourself productively; and feeling inadequate.

Being a child means being dependent upon your parents and following their rules. The same holds true for being a student and a member of society. But at some point, you must learn to provide for your own needs. This requires becoming aware of your needs.

What do you like to do in your spare time? Are you comfortable being alone? Do you like listening to music while studying, or do you prefer silence? Do you enjoy hanging out with many friends or just a few close ones? Does exercise relieve your stress?

Do you need a full night's sleep to avoid feeling irritable the next day?

The teen years can be intense, filled with competition and pressure to perform. For some this translates into thinking you are your grades, your looks or who you know. But honestly, external measures of success do not define you. You are a person with feelings and dreams.

Your parents may have expectations they wish for you to fulfill. Part of parenting means providing opportunities for children to experience new things and become self-sufficient. But if your parent wants you to be a doctor and you feel called to be a journalist, then a heartfelt discussion where you feel seen and heard needs to take place.

It takes great courage to be yourself without apology. It takes self-love to look in the mirror and see the precious individual that you are. It takes self-awareness to speak your own truth. These qualities are earned through making time to reflect upon who you are and where you want to go with your life.

 When I compare myself to models and actresses or even some of the girls at my school, I don't feel pretty. Sometimes when my weight goes up or my face breaks out or my hair won't do what I want it to, I feel ugly and even unhealthy. What can I do to change that and feel better about myself?

—Tiffany 16

 Do you know someone who looks beautiful on the outside, but is not a nice person? Do you know someone else who is not a beauty queen, but is funny and kind, someone you love to be around?

It's not uncommon for young women to compare themselves to the airbrushed images of actresses and models. Billboards, magazines and television are full of girls who appear flawless thanks to make-up artists, hair stylists, perfect lighting, good camera angles and photo shop. In reality, they have pimples and bad hair days just like you and me.

Each of us is born with our unique look. The size and shape of one's facial features as well as one's body shape is usually a combination of genetics. Thus we need to learn how to work with what we've got.

Have you noticed that people who eat fresh fruit and vegetables and drink plenty of water have clear skin and a healthy glow? People who exercise regularly have nice muscle tone and fit well in their clothes.

Before you decide to make any significant changes, ask yourself a couple of questions. Who are you changing for? Who are you comparing yourself to? What do you like about yourself? What can you realistically change?

If you decide to make some changes, make sure they come from a place of loving yourself. Your physical appearance is just a small part of who you really are. Hopefully, the people you choose to surround yourself with are wise enough to know this.

Ideally, your self-worth should be determined by how well your expression in the world aligns with your beliefs and vision for your life.

Sometimes I feel depressed even though nothing is really wrong. Other times I say or do things that I later regret. I used to be even tempered, and now I feel like my moods are out of control. Am I going crazy?

—Chloe, 17

 It is likely that what you are experiencing is a natural part of adolescence. Let me explain: Between the ages of 11 and 25, some pretty amazing changes occur in our bodies. On average, girls enter adolescence when their body reaches 17 percent body fat between ages 10 and 11.

During this transition the brain rewires itself for emotional attachment, reproduction, and ultimately, the creation of a stable family structure. Teens may experience a noticeable gap between intelligence and behavior, which experts used to attribute to the hormonal changes taking place, but there is actually a lot more going on in various parts of the brain at this time.

For one thing, the myelin sheathing that insulates nerves increases by 100 percent. Myelin sheathing is responsible for conducting nerve impulses to the brain. As the nerves become twice as efficient, the intensity and speed of reactions increase. Thus, the typical stereotype of impulsive teenage behavior — acting first, thinking later — leads to the common parent question: "What were you thinking?"

During the teen years, our bodies produce the lowest levels of serotonin in our lifetime. Serotonin, the primary transmitter in the limbic system, regulates morale and moods. These low serotonin levels create a state in which we can become susceptible to stress and overwhelm.

The brain doesn't grow in an orderly fashion. First it over-produces a multitude of connections that go to new parts of the brain, and then, beginning around age 16 through the mid-20s, it begins eliminating connections that are infrequently used. The connections that remain determine who we feel we are for the rest of our life. The human brain does not complete development until close to age 25 when the pre-frontal cortex, which is responsible for impulse control and functions like the director of a company, is fully developed.

So, if you find yourself saying and doing things you wish you hadn't, don't despair. Help is on the way — from your own brain.

 My grandmother died. I really loved her a lot and I miss her so much. I am afraid I might be turning into a Goth. It's not that I have nothing against them; it's just that I used to be happy and smile all the time. Now I feel bitter and cold. What should I do?

—Megan, 15

 I am truly sorry to hear about your grandmother dying. Saying goodbye to someone you love, and who has loved you, is bittersweet. The sadness you're feeling is because you've lost someone who brought love and delight into your life. The thought of not seeing her or speaking with her again just plain hurts, and you might continue to have those feelings for some time.

It's normal to feel bitter, even angry during this time. There is now an empty place where she once was, and it might leave you feeling less than enthused about other things you are involved in. You may also find that your sad feelings come in waves. Sometimes it may feel like you are drowning in them. Other times they may recede and just leave you feeling empty.

It is important to rest during this time, and take good care of yourself. Eat regular meals. Confide in someone you trust. This could be a good time to start a journal if you don't already have one. Feelings carry information for us, even the painful feelings. It is important to not run from your feelings, but to observe and learn from them. Your feelings about your grandmother's death are telling you about how much she meant to you.

You have just learned a very hard lesson about life: Nothing lasts forever. Humans — all living things — have a limited life span. This isn't something to be afraid of, but it can be very hard to comprehend and accept. This is why it is so very important to be grateful for the people we love and to tell them so.

Give yourself permission and time to grieve. Doing so does not mean you will never smile again.

I enjoy playing my guitar and writing songs about life and what I'm feeling. Sometimes I get so caught up in what I'm doing, I lose track of time and neglect my schoolwork. Is creating music a good use of my time, or should I only focus on school and things that will help me get into college?

—Chloe, 17

 Time spent in creative pursuits is never wasted. I am fascinated by how music can inspire and uplift us. I find that many of my teen clients use their music, writing, and art to express who they are and what is in their hearts. Self-expression is an important part of the human experience. Art, whether it is literature, music, poetry or dance, helps us connect meaningfully with others and ourselves.

In James Cameron's 2009 film "Avatar," the natives of a garden planet greet each other with the words "I see you." It was the deepest form of respect that one person could show another. They were saying, in essence, "I see you for who you really are." How often do you feel seen in this way?

Each of us has something unique to share with the world. If you are an artist, what are you doing to honor your gift of creative expression? Perhaps your music or writing will help someone else along his or her journey.

Not everyone is meant to be a performer or artist. Sometimes, being a good listener, or lending a helping hand can make all the difference in another person's life. Volunteering to assist others less fortunate is one of the most generous things you can do with your spare time.

If you are ever feeling bored or unhappy, being of service to others can give you an entirely new perspective. If you Google the name of your city along with "teen volunteer," you can find locations where you can participate. There are many varied ways to be of service that could also be a good match for your interests and talents.

We are all interdependent upon one another other. Someone else grows your food, makes your clothes, and builds your homes and schools. The teen years are a perfect time to begin reflecting upon how you would like to contribute to the world.

TAKING YOUR NEXT STEPS ...

How often do you stop to think about who you are and where you are going?

The willingness to learn more about yourself, your life's purpose and your place in the world is called self-reflection. This process helps you to understand why you might find certain situations difficult or unpleasant, and then come up with possible ways of dealing more effectively with similar experiences in the future.

Perhaps you will come to realize that there are certain skills you still need to learn. You might also come to recognize ways to avoid those situations in the future or how to turn them around. Self-reflection allows you to figure out more effective ways of being who and what you want to be in the world.

I wrote this survival guide as a jumping off point for a discussion about life and the value of talking to someone you trust. Parents are always good to turn to, when possible. But sometimes, it can also be helpful to turn to a neutral person, like a therapist, life coach, or mentor. The benefits of working with a teen life coach include:

• understanding and changing your self-defeating behaviors

- discovering your authentic self-expression
- enhancing your family relationships
- mastering your social interactions
- clarifying your dreams and goals
- improving your grades

Life coaching can be a fun and uplifting experience. In contrast to therapy, where the therapist is often seen as the expert, coaching is a collaborative effort between coach and client. The focus is on helping you to create a vision of the life you would like and then supporting you in your journey toward that goal.

If you live near Los Angeles, California, and would ever like to come in for a chat, just have your parents give me a call. My door is always open.

Here are some questions for you to reflect on:

1. As your body transitions from childhood to adulthood, are you reaching out to the more experienced women in your life -- mothers, siblings, aunts?

2. Do you sometimes have difficulty letting go of some friendships even though you realize it is probably time to move on?

3. Do you try too hard to please others and then end up feeling unhappy or anxious?

4. When choosing friends do you seek out the most popular

people, or do you prefer to find those with whom you can have an enjoyable conversation?

5. Are you honest and clear about who you are, or do you hide the most precious parts of yourself for fear of being hurt?

6. If you feel insulted, do you have the maturity to respond without attacking back?

7. Is expressing your truth easy for you, or do you often pretend to agree with your friends' opinions?

8. Instead of complaining and blaming others, do you take responsibility and turn a negative situation around?

9. Are you willing to settle for any guy just to have a boyfriend, or are you brave enough to keep looking for someone who is right for you?

10. While dreaming about what you may still want, how often do you express gratitude for what you already have?

11. How often do you compare yourself to others?

12. Do you find yourself making unsafe choices? If so, do you know why?

13. When someone says or does something that troubles you, do you initiate a talk that might clear the air?

14. Do you believe you have the right to be treated with kindness and respect?

15. Are you awkward around boys that you find attractive? If so, what are some things you can do to make yourself feel more comfortable?

16. Do you keep silent and let your boyfriend tell you what to do, or do you feel free to express your own ideas?

17. Are you likely to give in to peer pressure, or are you confident enough to listen to your own wisdom?

18. When you get dressed for school, do you always remember to put on a smile?

19. Is being "authentic" something common in your world or rare?

20. Do you change to please others or because the change makes sense to you?

21. Are you open to trying new experiences and meeting new people?

22. Do you get caught up in the popularity contest?

23. Are you in any relationships that intimidate you?

24. Are you aware when you are completely being yourself and when you are pretending to be someone else?

25. What is it about yourself that makes you feel proud?

26. What does your favorite song say about who you are?

27. If you were asked to write a story of your teen years, what key events would you include?

28. In years to come, when you look back on your life thus far, will you laugh, cry, feel embarrassed or proud?

29. What hope or thought carries you through challenging times?

30. Are you already living the life you want, or are you still waiting for your life to begin?

Journaling is another helpful way to gain insight into ourselves.

Sometimes it can seem like everyone else has it together while you alone are struggling. Did you know that keeping a journal is an excellent way to reflect on your experiences? This is incredibly important for understanding troubling or negative experiences.

Journaling allows you to explore what about a situation was unpleasant, and then to come up with possible ways of dealing more effectively with similar experiences in the future. You may come to realize that there are certain skills you still need to learn, ways to avoid those situations in the future, or how to turn them around.

Did you know that writing about emotional upheavals or difficulties you experience in daily life can actually improve physical and mental health? By recording and reflecting on your thoughts, you can gain insights, new perspectives, and enhance your mood.

To join my FREE online journaling community please visit my Web site at:

www.losangelesteentherapist.com

Sandra Dupont MA, MS, MFT
Teen Therapist & Life Coach
www.SandraDupontMFT.com
1421 Santa Monica Bl., Suite 108
Santa Monica, CA 90404
310.951.5678

ACKNOWLEDGEMENTS

I would like to acknowledge my father for always believing that I would someday write a book, Douglas Glenn Clark for encouraging me to do so, my sisters of the heart, Cameron James and Alison Roth for walking beside me in the process, and my beloved husband for his never-ending love and support.

COMING IN 2011

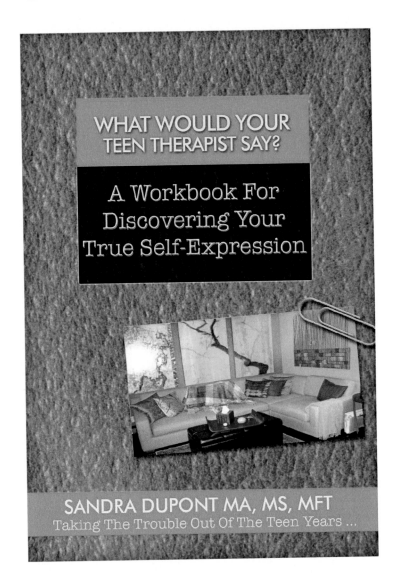

WHAT WOULD YOUR
TEEN THERAPIST SAY?

A Workbook For
Discovering Your
True Self-Expression

SANDRA DUPONT MA, MS, MFT
Taking The Trouble Out Of The Teen Years ...

Made in the USA
San Bernardino, CA
30 May 2016